T0394768

URSA

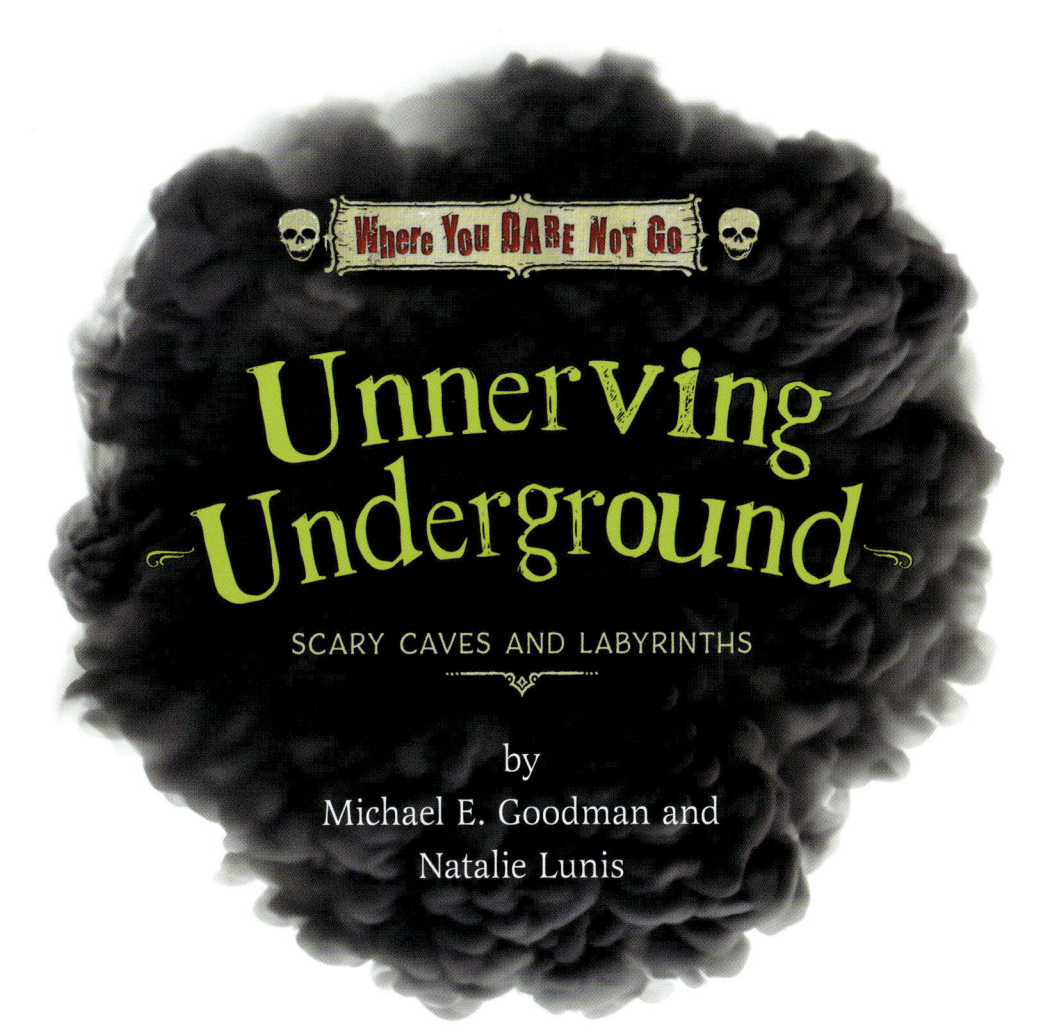

Where You DARE Not Go

Unnerving Underground

SCARY CAVES AND LABYRINTHS

by
Michael E. Goodman and
Natalie Lunis

BEARPORT
PUBLISHING

Minneapolis, Minnesota

Credits

Cover and title page, © Dedy Andrianto/iStock photo and © chokmoso/Adobe Stock and © Alan Liu/ Adobe Stock and © Ivan/Adobe Stock and © Gan/Adobe Stock ; 4–5, © Rodrigo/Adobe Stock and © Oriol Roca/Adobe Stock and © Cavan/Adobe Stock and © liskam/Adobe Stock; 6, © Www78/Wikimedia; 7TR, © Public domain/Wikimedia; 8, © DnDavis/Shutterstock; 9MR, © Pictures from History/Getty Images; 9BL, © fran_kie/Adobe Stock; 10, © Tbintb/Dreamstime; 11MR, © ana/Adobe Stock; 11BL, © gracious_ tiger/Shutterstock; 12, © SVPhilon/iStock photo; 13TR, © Hercules Milas/Alamy Stock Photo; 13BL, © natalia_maroz/Shutterstock; 14, © Amy Gillung/Shutterstock; 15TR, © Public domain/Wikimedia; 15BL, © Maxal Tamor/Adobe Stock; 16, © Andriana Syvanych/Shutterstock; 17TR, © Poland-01508 - Hard Work/Wikimedia; 17MR, © Barbara Maliszewska/Wikimedia; 18, © Golden Ratio Photos/Shutterstock; 19BL, © Domnitsky Yaroslav/Adobe Stock; 20, © Brian Logan Photography/Shutterstock; 21BL, © Johnny Madsen/Alamy Stock Photo; 22, © Wangkun Jia/Shutterstock; 23BR, © New York Daily News Archive/ Getty Images; 24, © Public domain/Wikimedia; 25BL, © Danita Delimont/Alamy Stock Photo; 26, © CJH Photography/Adobe Stock; 27BR, © lotosfoto/Adobe Stock; 28, © Gubin Yury/Shutterstock; 29TR, © Public domain/Wikimedia; 30, © Fiona M. Donnelly/Shutterstock; 31TR, © Public domain/Wikimedia; 31BR, © Fiona M. Donnelly/Shutterstock; 32, © Ulrich Baumgarten/Getty Images; 33BR, © Ulrich Baumgarten/ Getty Images; 34, © Cavan Images/Alamy Stock Photo; 34MR, © Kumar Sriskandan/Alamy Stock Photo; 35BL, © Luigi Petro/Alamy Stock Photo; 36, © gary yim/Shutterstock; 37BL, © Shaun Jeffers/Shutterstock; 38, © Kjetil Bjørnsrud/Wikimedia; 40, © Wyco/iStock photo; 41MR, © Cassowary Colorizations/Wikimedia; 41BL, © Kev Gregory/Shutterstock; 42–43, © Triff/Shutterstock

Bearport Publishing Company Product Development Team

Publisher: Jen Jenson; Director of Product Development: Spencer Brinker; Managing Editor: Allison Juda; Editor: Cole Nelson; Associate Editor: Naomi Reich; Associate Editor: Tiana Tran; Designer: Kim Jones; Designer: Kayla Eggert; Designer: Steve Scheluchin; Production Specialist: Owen Hamlin

Statement on Usage of Generative Artificial Intelligence

Bearport Publishing remains committed to publishing high-quality nonfiction books. Therefore, we restrict the use of generative AI to ensure accuracy of all text and visual components pertaining to a book's subject. See BearportPublishing.com for details.

Library of Congress Cataloging-in-Publication Data is available at www.loc.gov or upon request from the publisher.

ISBN: 979-8-89577-095-5 (hardcover)
ISBN: 979-8-89577-212-6 (ebook)

For more information, write to Bearport Publishing, 5357 Penn Avenue South, Minneapolis, MN 55419.

Contents

Fear from Below

On a beautiful day, the sun shines down and birds sing while a fresh breeze blows. But what about below? Deep underground lie caverns, labyrinths, and lost cities . . . just waiting for visitors from above. Would you dare travel to these ghost-filled places below?

A Witchy Ghost

The Bell Witch is one of America's most famous ghosts—and also one of the fiercest. This spirit once caused all kinds of trouble for a family living on a Tennessee farm. It wasn't long, however, until visitors to a nearby cave could also feel the witch's fury.

The entrance to the Bell Witch Cave

6

In the early 1800s, a settler named John Bell moved with his family to northern Tennessee. The Bells worked hard to build a house and start a farm. Then, in 1817, horrible problems began.

The Bell family house

Inside the house, the Bells heard knocking and scratching noises. Then, bedsheets were pulled off sleeping children and guests. Family members were slapped and had their hair pulled by an unseen force. After a while, the ghost started talking, revealing to them that its name was Kate. People thought the angry spirit must be a witch sent by Kate Batts, a neighbor who had once had an argument over money with John Bell.

In 1821, about a year after John's death, the spirit left the Bell home, but she didn't go far. Since that time, her presence has often been felt in a nearby cave—now called the Bell Witch Cave. If reports are true, the witch still has a temper. She has been said to grab, pin down, and slap people who go on the underground tour— especially those who dare to express any doubts that she exists. ⚬

Once, a group of teenagers visited the Bell Witch Cave. After complaining that they hadn't seen any ghosts, one girl was pushed to the ground by an unseen force. She then felt a slap. When the tour guide shined a light on her face, everyone could see red marks that looked like they were made from the fingers of a hand.

An Army Made of Clay

In 1974, there was almost no rain in Xi'an (SHEE-ahn), China. Crops were dying. Farmers knew the only way to save their farms was to dig a well to get water from the ground. Digging a well, however, terrified them. According to an old legend, there were ghosts hiding under the fields in Xi'an—the ghosts of ancient Chinese soldiers. In a strange way, the legend was true.

The terra-cotta soldiers

Desperate for water, the farmers of Xi'an began to dig a well despite the stories saying the ground beneath them was haunted. They didn't find ghosts, however. What they found instead was a head and arm made out of terra-cotta, a kind of clay. When archaeologists heard about the discovery, they came to Xi'an and unearthed an entire underground palace with secret rooms connected by dark, winding tunnels. Some of the rooms were filled with life-size clay soldiers that were more than 2,000 years old.

Who had built the ancient labyrinth, and why? The archaeologists concluded that it had been created around 215 BCE by Shi Huang (SHEE WONG), who became the first emperor of China at age 13. Although the young emperor was powerful, he was also afraid of death. As a result, he soon began building his own tomb. Over time, it would grow to become a sprawling underground city, complete with a clay army to stand guard and protect the emperor's spirit in the afterlife.

Emperor Shi Huang

It took 700,000 men more than 30 years to complete the labyrinth. To protect the tomb's secrets after the emperor died, the tomb's architects were sealed inside. No one escaped alive.

A Ghost of the Civil War

Do some ghosts haunt the places where their lives were lost? That may be true for one soldier. He is said to have remained in a Tennessee cave long after the war he was fighting in ended.

Inside Craighead Caverns

For a long time, a series of caves now known as Craighead Caverns served as shelter for Cherokee Indians. These first discoverers of the caves left behind a rich assortment of belongings, including arrowheads, jewelry, and pottery. Later, in the 1820s, the first white settlers in the area started using the caves in a different way. They stored potatoes and other foods inside the cool underground spaces.

During the U.S. Civil War (1861–1865), the caves served yet another purpose. Deep inside, Confederate soldiers dug for saltpeter, a rock salt used to make gunpowder. According to a diary that one of the soldiers left behind, a Union spy discovered the mine and tried to blow it up. However, the Northern soldier was captured and shot just outside the cave entrance before he could carry out his plan. Since that time, some say his ghost has been spotted inside Craighead Caverns—one more piece of history that has been left behind in the deep, dark caves.

The Lost Sea

The largest underground lake in the United States, known as the Lost Sea, lies deep within Craighead Caverns. The 4.5-acre (1.8-ha) lake was discovered by a 13-year-old boy in 1905—exactly 40 years after the Civil War ended.

A Place to Hide and Pray

In 1963, a man knocking down a wall inside a cave in central Turkey made an amazing find. He discovered a huge underground city—Derinkuyu (*der*-in-KOO-yoo)—that had been forgotten for centuries. The city got its start more than 2,500 years ago, when people began to dig tunnellike labyrinths in the soft layer of rock that lay below their towns. They hollowed out long hallways and secret rooms where they could hide when enemies attacked.

Entrance to the underground city of Derinkuyu

Over the centuries, as ancient townspeople continued to dig, the labyrinths of Derinkuyu became larger and larger—so large, in fact, that they came to form a small underground city. The city has 50 tunnels and its own river. Its longest passageway stretches 5.6 miles (9 km) and connects to another underground city, called Kaymakli.

A stone door

Long ago, Derinkuyu had everything people needed to survive for months. Since parts of the city extended as deep as 278 feet (85 m) underground, its most important feature was a system of ventilation shafts that provided air from above. Derinkuyu also included kitchens, storage rooms, stables, and even schools and churches. Thick stone doors were used to seal off the entrances to each level of the city. Once they were in place, the people underground were safely hidden. ⌇⌇

A passageway inside the underground city

The incredible underground world of Derinkuyu is thought to have been able to house as many as 100,000 people.

13

The Pennsylvania Hermit

A story from Pennsylvania's history tells of a hermit who wandered the countryside and then lived the last 19 years of his life in a cave. Who was this man, and why would he choose to spend so much time in such a dark, lonely place?

Inside Indian Echo Caverns

William Wilson and his younger sister, Elizabeth, were born on a farm not far from Philadelphia in the 1760s. In 1785, at the age of 20 or so, Elizabeth was accused of murder, found guilty, and sentenced to hang. William, who was working as a stone carver in another town, heard what had happened and tried hard to get her freed. He gathered evidence of Elizabeth's innocence and received a pardon for her. Tragically, however, he arrived at the execution minutes too late—Elizabeth had already been hanged.

William Wilson

William never got over his sister's death. He wandered through parts of Pennsylvania for 17 years and then reached a hilly area with many caves. He finally settled down in one of them and lived there all alone until his death in 1821. According to some versions of the story, even then he was unable to find peace, and his ghost has haunted the cave ever since. Other stories say that two lonely spirits have been spotted wandering throughout the caverns. Could they be brother and sister, reunited at last?

William Wilson was known to have only a few simple belongings inside the cave. These included a straw mattress, a table and stool, a pot for cooking, and a few books.

Surrounded by Salt

Before refrigerators, salt was used to keep food from spoiling. It was so valuable that it was known as white gold. The precious substance was produced either from seawater or from rock that had to be dug from deep within the earth. In Wieliczka (vee-LEETS-kuh), workers have been mining salt for more than 700 years. In that time, they have also created an eerie wonderland deep underground.

Life-size salt statues in the mine depict a local legend.

The Wieliczka Salt Mine is massive, reaching 186 miles (300 km) in length and extending as deep as 1,073 ft. (327 m) belowground. It includes several underground lakes and nine levels of passageways, galleries, and chambers. One of the most amazing chambers is Saint Kinga's Chapel, which has been a place of worship since about 1896. Lit by huge chandeliers made with glass-like salt crystals, the chapel has an altar, statues, and detailed images carved from rock salt.

A model of what it was like to work in the salt mines

Three miners created the chapel over a period of 68 years. Since mining is a dangerous job, these underground workers wanted places to pray. Methane gas builds up in mines and can be easily ignited by a spark, a lamp, or other fire source. As many as 2,000 workers in the Wieliczka Salt Mine faced the possibility of an explosion every day they worked. ⟳

According to legend, a ghost often appeared before disasters occurred in the Wieliczka Salt Mine and warned miners with the words, "Do not go."

The Guide Who Wouldn't Leave

Caves aren't always creepy and scary—they can also be beautiful. That's what people living in Marengo, Indiana, found out after two children discovered a huge cave just outside town. One tour guide loved the cave so much that he found it hard to stay away—even after his death.

Marengo Cave

One September day in 1883, 15-year-old Blanche Hiestand and her younger brother, Orris, went out exploring. They made their way down an opening in the ground and were stunned by what they found. The opening led to a huge underground chamber filled with shimmering rock formations.

The owner of the property was sure that people would pay to see these underground wonders, and he soon began offering tours of the cave. By far, the most dedicated guide ever to lead the tours was a man named Bill Clifton. For more than 50 years, Clifton took visitors through Marengo Cave no matter how early or late in the day they arrived. When he retired in 1965 at the age of 79, he continued to live nearby.

After Clifton's death in 1980, people who entered the caves started noticing strange things. One guide heard the entrance door slam shut—even though no one had come in. People on tours have heard both singing and rhythmic tapping. Are there natural explanations for these happenings? Or are they signs that Bill Clifton never left the cave he knew and loved so well?

During the time the cave has been open to the public, weddings, dances, and theater performances have taken place inside. At one wedding, it is said that Bill Clifton provided music by tapping on different parts of the cave with a wooden hammer.

The Labyrinth of Courage

During World War II (1939–1945), Budapest (BOO-duh-*pest*) was invaded, and Russian tanks roared through the streets. Frightened people scattered during each attack, searching for safety. Thousands of them made their way to a hilly part of the city. There, they entered Buda Castle to reach the underground tunnels and caves nicknamed the Labyrinth of Courage.

Buda Castle

The Labyrinth of Courage is millions of years old. It was created by rivers of hot water that pushed through layers of rock. The rushing water carved out a group of more than 200 tunnels, which underground workers later connected.

Long before World War II, people started using the tunnels as hiding places. In fact, scientists believe ancient cave dwellers may have been the first to do so, using the tunnels to escape from wild animals half a million years ago. Much later, after a bloody invasion by Mongols in the 13th century, the people of Hungary built Buda Castle on top of the labyrinth. The web of tunnels provided a place of safety for castle dwellers during times of battle. Finally, in the 20th century, the labyrinth became a shelter capable of housing 10,000 people—offering a place to escape from the violence and destruction of World War II.

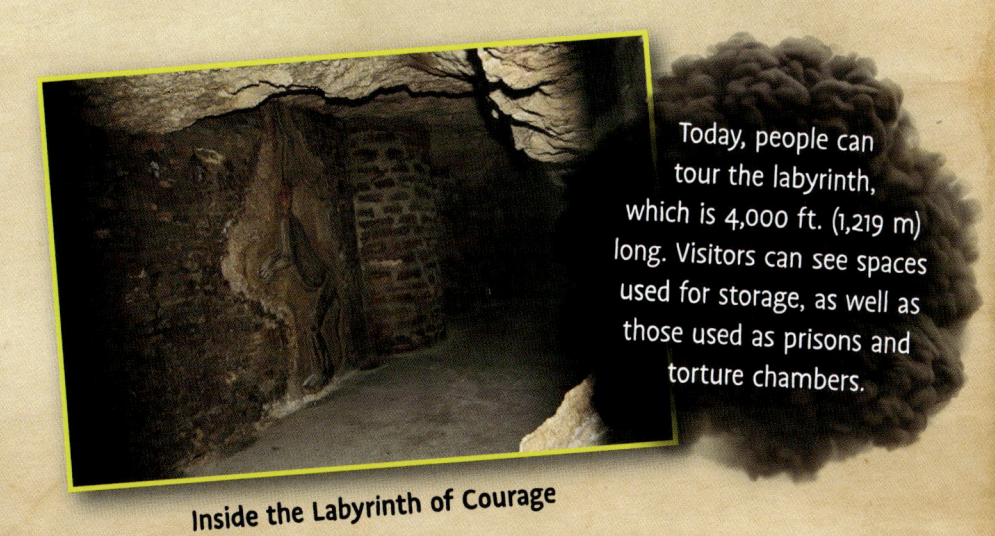

Today, people can tour the labyrinth, which is 4,000 ft. (1,219 m) long. Visitors can see spaces used for storage, as well as those used as prisons and torture chambers.

Inside the Labyrinth of Courage

Trapped Forever?

Floyd Collins was born near Mammoth Cave, the largest cave system in the world. While he was growing up in the early 1900s, several parts were famous as show caves, where tickets were sold and tours were offered. Collins wanted to find new underground areas that would bring in money for his family. Unfortunately, he ended up paying a huge price for trying to make such a discovery.

The historic entrance to Mammoth Cave National Park

In 1917, Floyd Collins discovered a show cave that became known as Crystal Cave. In 1925, eager for more discoveries, he started exploring a small passageway called Sand Cave. While crawling through a narrow area on his belly, Collins loosened a large, heavy rock that fell and pinned his ankle so that he could not move. Rescue crews found him, but because of the narrowness of the spot, no one could reach him. After being trapped underground for about 15 days, Collins died.

In the years following the deadly accident, stories about the explorer's ghost began to appear. An especially chilling one traces back to 1976, when two workers were checking water levels near Sand Cave. One of them heard the voice of a man, but it was not that of his partner. The voice called out, "Help me! Help me, I'm trapped! Johnny, help me!" Eerily, the last person Floyd Collins had spoken to before becoming trapped was a friend—whose name was Johnny Gerald.

The attempt to rescue Floyd Collins became a huge news story. Reporters from all over the country camped out near the entrance to Sand Cave. One newspaper writer, Skeets Miller, even crawled into the cave several times to interview the trapped man.

Outside the cave, people used special instruments to try to hear whether Floyd Collins's heart was still beating.

Ghost Town Underground

The neighborhood in Seattle called Pioneer Square was built on muddy, flat land. When the tide was very high in the nearby inlet, water often flooded the buildings and sewers backed up, causing toilets to spew like fountains. Then, in 1889, a fire burned out of control and destroyed most of the neighborhood's structures. When Pioneer Square was rebuilt, the builders accidentally created an underground ghost town.

Pioneer Square after the fire

To escape the mud and damage caused by floods, the new streets of Pioneer Square were built between 12 ft. (3.7 m) and 30 ft. (9.1 m) higher than the old ones. This meant that buildings not destroyed by the fire were now nearly hidden underground and were connected by a winding labyrinth of dark, dirty streets. By 1907, most of the underground area was abandoned because of rats and disease. Although the people left, some say ghosts have stayed behind.

According to stories, the ghosts are of people who had lived or worked in the area before the fire. Some people say one ghost is a bank teller who nervously walks back and forth, worried about all the gold he has to guard. Others tell of seeing a ghost sitting and staring sadly at the stage of an old theater. They say the spirit had suffered a painful death when stage lights fell on him during a play.

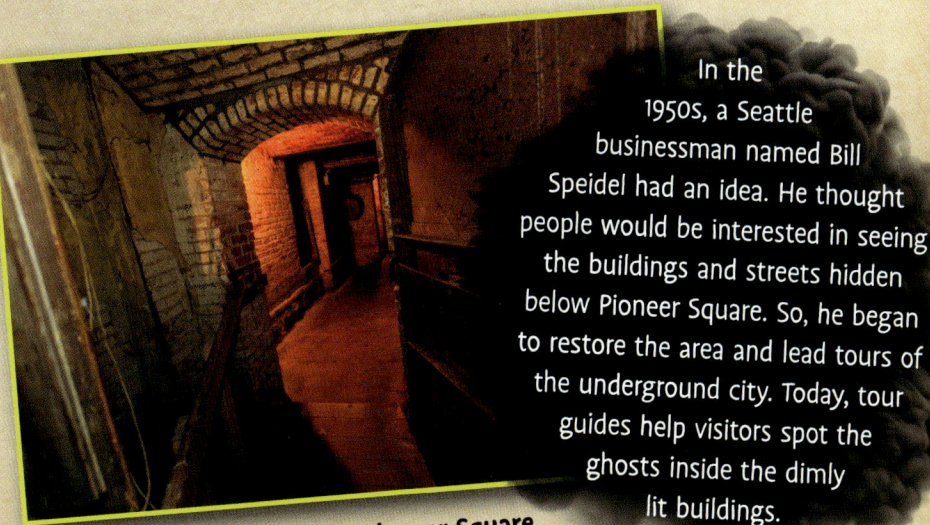

A passageway under Pioneer Square

In the 1950s, a Seattle businessman named Bill Speidel had an idea. He thought people would be interested in seeing the buildings and streets hidden below Pioneer Square. So, he began to restore the area and lead tours of the underground city. Today, tour guides help visitors spot the ghosts inside the dimly lit buildings.

Send In the Ghost Hunters

FANTASTIC CAVERNS
SPRINGFIELD, MISSOURI

Many ghosts have well-known histories. Some, however, are more mysterious. When a spirit's identity is unknown, ghost hunters are sometimes called in. That's what happened in one Missouri cave, where a girl in a polka-dot dress has appeared—for reasons no one can explain.

The entrance to Fantastic Caverns

In 1862, a Missouri farmer named John Knox went out hunting with his dog. Together, the two discovered the entrance to a deep set of caverns. A few years later, Knox placed an ad in a newspaper inviting volunteers to explore the cave. Twelve women from the Springfield Women's Athletic Club stepped up to the challenge. They arrived with supplies and entered the caves. Once there, they carved their initials into the rock, leaving a reminder of their visit.

During the 1950s, the cave was named Fantastic Caverns and opened for tours. Since that time, many strange sights have been reported, including a ghostly girl in a polka-dot dress.

To learn more about the possible haunting, the cave's owners allowed ghost hunters—people who track down spirits—to investigate the caves. So far, however, the case is still unsolved. The experts have not been able to figure out who the girl in the polka-dot dress is—or rather, who she *was*. ⤳

People have found strange glowing shapes in photos they took while visiting Fantastic Caverns. Ghost hunters call these shapes orbs. Orbs often appear in photos taken in places thought to be haunted.

27

The Secret Subway

Every day, people who live in the city of Moscow take the Metro to work. Little do many of them know, however, the Metro may not be the city's only subway system. Though the government denies its existence, a mystery subway, the Metro 2, is said to exist 164 to 656 ft. (50 to 200 m) belowground. Why is this labyrinth such a big secret?

The Moscow Metro

28

If accounts about Moscow's secret subway are true, work on Metro 2 began during World War II, when German troops were marching toward Moscow. During this time of great fear, the Soviet Union's powerful leader, Joseph Stalin, considered destroying the Metro so the Germans couldn't capture and use it. However, he changed his mind and kept the trains running. Then—according to reports—he ordered a secret labyrinth to be dug far below the original Metro. He planned to build a hidden subway system there that would be able to take Soviet leaders out of Moscow if the Germans captured the city.

Joseph Stalin

In the early 1950s, Stalin would have had another purpose for Metro 2. It would have served as a bomb shelter if nuclear war broke out between his country and the United States. Supposedly, work on Metro 2 stopped after Stalin died in 1953, but some of the tunnels are still around, locked away and hidden. As far as most people know, Metro 2 hasn't been finished and was never used for train travel.

If Metro 2 indeed exists, most of the workers who built it must have been women. Why? Most of the city's men were in the Soviet army, fighting in World War II.

The Stolen Heart

Many caves were carved out by natural forces, such as flowing water from rivers. Some, however, were dug by people for purposes such as mining or making a shelter. One famous set of caves was even created to serve as a meeting place for English gentlemen. These human-made caves may not be as old as those carved out by nature, but they can be just as haunted.

The entrance to Hellfire Caves

Hellfire Caves have been open to visitors since 1951. More than two million people have toured them.

The Hellfire Caves were named after the Hell-Fire Club—a group that met there during the mid-1700s. The founder of the club, Sir Francis Dashwood, hired local workers to dig a series of underground rooms out of a hill near his family's home. He then invited his closest friends—who happened to be some of the richest and most powerful men in England—to join him for meetings and fancy dinners in the cave's elegantly decorated chambers.

Sir Francis Dashwood

Some people say that one of the members of the club, Paul Whitehead, never left the caves. When he died in 1774, Whitehead left some money to Sir Francis. The money was to be used to buy an urn—in which Whitehead's heart was to be kept, always at his beloved club. Sir Francis honored his friend's wishes, until someone stole the heart during the 1820s. The urn, however, was left behind and kept in the caves, where it can still be seen by visitors. According to some, Whitehead's ghost can also be seen—perhaps forever searching for his lost heart. ♈

Inside Hellfire Caves

America's Fortress

In a human-made labyrinth 2,000 ft. (610 m) inside a Colorado mountain, government workers scan computer screens day and night. Satellites that track the skies around Earth beam information to computers inside the mountain's labyrinth 24 hours a day, 7 days a week. If something flashes across the screens, the operators need to decide whether or not it poses a threat. If it does, they must act quickly since millions of U.S. citizens may be at risk.

The entrance to Cheyenne Mountain

CHEYENNE MOUNTAIN COMPLEX

In 1979, a training program showing a pretend attack was accidentally run on the Cheyenne computers. This caused a warning message to be sent to U.S. Air Force bases around the world. At least 10 fighter planes were launched to patrol the skies.

The labyrinth inside Cheyenne Mountain was built in the 1960s to help the United States survive in the event of a nuclear war. The entrance has 2 doors that are 25 tons (23 t) each. They are so well made that even though they're very heavy, only two people are needed to push the doors open. Inside the mountain, there are 15 buildings set on more than 1,000 springs. The springs will prevent the buildings from collapsing if the fortress is hit by earthquakes or a nuclear explosion. The operation center can withstand a 30-megaton bomb blast. Water is held in underground reservoirs that are so large, it takes a rowboat to cross them.

The computer system in the labyrinth is set up to warn the U.S. Air Force of enemy missile attacks. When the computers show something in the air, operators must quickly determine if it is space junk, other debris moving through the sky, or a true threat to the United States.

Operators working at their computers

A Deep, Dark Shelter

⟶ CHISLEHURST CAVES ⟵
BROMLEY, ENGLAND

Thousands of years ago, before people started building towns and cities, early humans in some parts of the world used caves for shelter. Surprisingly, in modern times, people have also found refuge in these spaces carved out of the earth.

The Haunted Pool in Chislehurst Caves

A map of the caves

Chislehurst Caves, located just outside London, were not formed by nature. The history of the caves, however, goes back further than many other human-made caves—about 5,000 years. The people who created and worked inside the caves used them for mining both flint, a hard rock used to make tools and simple weapons, and chalk, a soft rock used to make plaster.

During World War II, English men, women, and children living nearby moved into the caves to escape the bombs being dropped by German planes. At one point, as many as 15,000 people were using the space as a huge air raid shelter, sleeping in bunk beds that had been built for this special purpose. There were even two churches and a hospital set up within the caves.

Nowadays, the caves are open for tours, as well as for parties. During these events, however, tourists and partygoers sometimes hear strange noises—most often footsteps or the voices of children. Are these the sounds of spirits, reminding today's visitors of the caves' long and unusual history?

Mannequins of a family

During the tour of Chislehurst Caves, visitors see mannequins dressed and posed to show how people who used the caves during World War II would have lived.

The Worms Crawl In

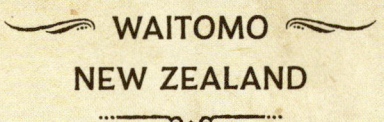
For nearly 1,000 years, the Māori people of New Zealand told stories about glittering stars shining inside an underground cave. This legendary place was called Waitomo (whye-TOH-moh), which means water hole in the Māori language. For years, the only known way to enter the cave was through an underground stream that flowed from one pitch-black tunnel to another. Who would brave the darkness for a chance to reach the stars?

A modern entrance to Waitomo caves

In 1887, a Māori chief named Tane Tinorau (TAH-nay TIN-or-oo) and a British man named Fred Mace decided to paddle into Waitomo. They built a small raft out of reeds, a type of tall grass. They passed through several dark tunnels and then entered an open underground room. Above them, the low ceiling was covered with tiny lights. They put out their torches and reached up to the ceiling to touch what looked like stars. That's when they discovered the secret of Waitomo.

The lights in the ceiling of the cave were actually thousands of glowworms! These little creatures give off a soft blue light to attract the bugs they eat. The explorers backed out of the room carefully and paddled out to tell others what they had found. Today, descendants of Tane Tinorau guide visitors through the caverns filled with oozing, drippy, glowing worms.

Light produced by living things, such as glowworms, is known as bioluminescence.

The glowworms are not the only special feature of the caves. The largest room inside, called the Cathedral, has great acoustics. That means it is an excellent place to perform or hear music. Several famous singers have come to Waitomo to fill the dimly lit caves with beautiful music.

Life—and Death—Underground

Edinburgh, Scotland, is said to be one of the most haunted cities in the world. But one of the city's most haunted places is especially chilling. This cluster of human-made caves were once part of a huge stone bridge.

Vaults in the South Bridge

In the late 1700s, space was hard to find in the busy city of Edinburgh. As a result, people put up buildings on top of South Bridge, a huge stone structure featuring 19 openings, or arches. The arches—that had now become underground spaces—were also put to use. Business owners put in floors and ceilings to create many small rooms, known as vaults, which could be used for storage and as workshops.

After only a few years, water began to seep into the vaults, and they were abandoned when this resulted in floods. At that point, the city's poorest residents moved in, making homes out of the cold, damp, dark spaces. Crime, disease, and death were common in these cramped urban caves, and after about 50 years, the vaults were once again abandoned.

The South Bridge Vaults were forgotten until the 1980s, when they were rediscovered and opened up for tours. Not surprisingly, there have since been many reports of ghostly activity in this place that was once so dirty, dangerous, and deadly. Among the vaults' most famous ghosts is a boy known as Jack, who is reported to grab the hands of unsuspecting visitors.

Several of the ghosts said to haunt the South Bridge Vaults have become well known in Edinburgh, including an angry spirit named Mr. Boots. People claim he pushes visitors and throws rocks at them.

Ghosts in the Tube

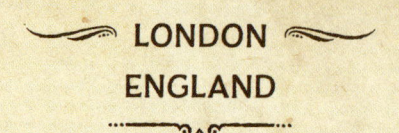

The world's first subway system, the Tube, opened in London in 1863. The idea of building anything underground frightened some people at the time. A minister in one London church warned it could allow the devil to escape from the underworld. Since the Tube was built, no one has seen the devil below London. However, some people say they have seen ghosts.

The abandoned
Aldwych station

In the nearly 150 years since it opened, many people have died in the Tube, also known as the London Underground. Trains have crashed, people have been murdered, fires have broken out, and stations have been bombed. In addition, while workers dug the original tunnels, many graves were disturbed. The Aldgate station, for example, was built in the middle of a mass grave where 1,000 people were buried during the plague of 1665.

With so much death, it's no wonder that ghosts have been seen in so many of the stations. Some people claim that the ghost of a dead actor still performs in Aldwych station, where a theater once stood. Another station, Covent Garden, is said to be haunted by the actor William "Breezy Bill" Terriss, who was stabbed to death in 1897. As he lay dying, he was heard to say, "I'll be back." Since then, Breezy Bill has been spotted in a gray suit and white gloves, waiting for the train.

William "Breezy Bill" Terriss

Not all ghosts that haunt the Tube are people. In 1928, a passenger on a train passing through South Kensington station heard a loud, piercing train whistle. He then watched an entire ghost train appear and disappear in front of him.

The World of the . . .

An underground ghost town in Seattle, Washington

Glowing shapes in Springfield, Missouri

An eternal tour guide in Marengo, Indiana

A mourning hermit in Hummelstown, Pennsylvania

A nuclear bomb shelter in Colorado Springs, Colorado

A violent witch in Adams, Tennessee

A trapped man in Mammoth Cave, Kentucky

A Union ghost in Sweetwater, Tennessee

PACIFIC OCEAN

NORTH AMERICA

ATLANTIC OCEAN

SOUTH AMERICA

N
W E
S

SOUTHERN OCEAN

Unnerving Underground

ARCTIC OCEAN

Forgotten vaults in Edinburgh, Scotland

A heartless spirit in West Wycombe, England

An abandoned shelter in Bromley, England

A secret subway in Moscow, Russia

ASIA

EUROPE

Haunted salt mines in Wieliczka, Poland

Clay soldiers in Xi'an, China

A ghost train in London, England

The Labyrinth of Courage in Budapest, Hungary

An underground city in Derinkuyu, Turkey

PACIFIC OCEAN

AFRICA

INDIAN OCEAN

AUSTRALIA

Glowing worms in Waitomo, New Zealand

Glossary

acoustics how well sound can be carried or heard in a room

afterlife a person's existence after he or she has died

air raid shelter a place people go to find safety during a bombing from the air

archaeologists scientists who learn about ancient times by studying artifacts, such as old buildings and tools

architects people who design buildings and make sure they are built properly

caverns another word for caves

cave system a set of connected caves

chamber a closed-in space

chandeliers fancy light fixtures that hang from ceilings

chapel a building or room used for praying

Civil War the U.S. war between the Southern states and the Northern states, which lasted from 1861 to 1865

Confederate soldiers people who fought for the Southern states during the U.S. Civil War

dedicated loyal

execution punishment by death

fury anger

gunpowder an explosive mixture used in guns and cannons

hermit a person who lives alone and hides away from the rest of the world

inlet a narrow body of water running from a larger body of water, such as an ocean, into land

labyrinth a set of winding, connected pathways in which it is easy to get lost

legend a story that has been passed down from long ago that may be based on fact but is not always completely true

linger to stay longer than expected

mannequins life-size dummies

Māori Indigenous people of New Zealand

megaton the explosive force of 1,000,000 tn. (910,000 t) of dynamite

methane gas a colorless, odorless, flammable gas often found in mines

mine a deep hole or tunnel from which rock or other materials are taken

missile a weapon that is able to fly a great distance to reach its target

Mongols people from the Mongol Empire, which stretched through Asia and parts of Europe during the 1200s and 1300s

nuclear having to do with the type of energy produced by splitting atoms

pardon release from punishment

plague a disease that spreads quickly and often kills many people

refuge safety and protection

reservoirs natural or artificial holding areas for storing water

retired stopped working

rock formations rocks that have special shapes

rock salt salt found in solid form as a mineral

satellites spacecraft that are sent into outer space to gather and send back information to Earth

settler a person who makes a home in a new place

spirit world the world of supernatural creatures, such as ghosts

sprawling vast and spread out

temper a tendency to get angry

tomb a grave, room, or building designed to house a dead body

Union soldier a person who fought for the Northern states during the U.S. Civil War

urban having to do with cities

urn a large vase with a base

vaults places, sometimes dug into the ground, for keeping or protecting things

ventilation shafts passageways that allow fresh air into an area and stale air out

World War II a worldwide conflict that involved many countries and lasted from 1939 to 1945

Read More

Gagne, Tammy. *The Haunted History of Alcatraz Island (Haunted History of the United States).* Minneapolis: ABDO Publishing, 2024.

Markovics, Joyce L. and Dinah Williams. *Petrifying Playtime: Scary Amusement Parks and Playgrounds (Where You Dare Not Go).* Minneapolis: Bearport Publishing Company, 2025.

Sheen, Barbara. *Ghosts and Spirits (Exploring the Occult).* San Diego: ReferencePoint Press, 2024.

Learn More Online

1. Go to **FactSurfer.com** or scan the QR code below.

2. Enter "**Unnerving Underground**" into the search box.

3. Click on the cover of this book to see a list of websites.

~ Index ~

Where do you
dare NOT go?